★American★Girl Library™

HELP!

An absolutely indispensable Guide to Life FOR GIRLS!

By Nancy Holyoke
Illustrated by Scott Nash

PLEASANT COMPANY

Published by Pleasant Company Publications
© Copyright 1995 by Pleasant Company
All rights reserved. No part of this book may be used or reproduced
in any manner whatsoever without written permission except
in the case of brief quotations embodied in critical articles and reviews.
For information, address: Book Editor, Pleasant Company Publications,
8400 Fairway Place, P.O. Box 620998, Middleton, WI 53562.

First Edition.
Printed in the United States of America.
96 97 98 99 KRH 10 9 8 7 6 5 4

American Girl Library™ is a trademark of Pleasant Company.

Editorial Development by Peggy Ross, Jeanette Wall, and Roberta Johnson
Art Direction by Kym Abrams and Jane S. Varda

Library of Congress Cataloging-in-Publication Data

Holyoke, Nancy.
"Help!" : an absolutely indispensable guide to life for girls / by Nancy Holyoke ;
illustrated by Scott Nash. — 1st ed.
p.   cm.
Summary: Presents letters written to "American Girl" magazine
by girls asking for advice about the problems they face in everyday life.

ISBN 1-56247-230-5 (pbk.)
1. Girls—United States—Life skills guides. 2. Girls—United States—Conduct of life.
[1. Conduct of life.   2. Letters.]   I. Title.
HQ777.H64   1995   070.4´44—dc20   95-7656   CIP   AC

Dear Reader,

Every month, *American Girl* magazine receives over 1,300 letters from girls asking for advice about the problems they face in everyday life. This book is made up of just a few of those letters.

The letters are about friends. They're about families. They're about feelings—fears and frustrations, anger and love.

True friends listen closely and answer honestly, and that's what we've tried to do in this book. We hope you'll find advice that you can use.

We also hope you'll remember the girls you meet here. Why? Because your school is full of girls just like them—and they could use a kind word from a girl just like *you*.

Your friends at *American Girl*

Afraid of the Dark

Dear *Help!*,

I'm scared of the dark. I try every-thing in my power not to be. I put the lights on. I listen to the radio. I even go in and sleep with my parents. Sometimes I keep the whole house awake at two in the morning. Help me, please!

Christy

Think: Do you do anything during the day that causes you grief at night? Do you watch scary shows? Do you eat or drink things with a lot of sugar or caffeine after dinner? Changing habits like these can be a big, big help. Also, if you find that something gives you comfort, make it part of your routine. Turn on a night-light and radio *before* the panic starts. Try talking out loud to yourself, too. The sound of your own voice, reciting a poem or singing a song, can make you feel calmer. You'll soon believe what you've always known: there's nothing under your bed but dirty socks.

Babysitting

My mom just said she is giving me her permission to babysit. She talked to my aunt and told her I would be available. Now what do I do?

Baby Lover

1. Study up.
Spend an evening with your cousins while your aunt is at home. Watch what she does. You'll learn a lot! You might also call your local American Red Cross and ask about babysitting classes. A class can teach you how to take care of babies, handle emergencies, and lots more.

2. Be a businesswoman.
What do other girls your age charge to babysit in your town? Find out, and set your own rates. You might also want to advertise your service to neighbors through flyers or phone calls.

3. Be prompt.
When you land a job, plan ahead about how to get there, and *be on time*.

4. Know the territory.
What are the rules for bedtime? Meals? TV? Where are the diapers and the favorite toys? Ask questions before the parents go, while you have the chance.

5. Write down phone numbers.

Most parents will leave a note about where they're going and include a phone number where they can be reached. If they don't, ask! You should have local emergency numbers, too.

6. Watch the kids, not the TV.

You're there to keep the children safe, and for little kids in particular that means never letting them out of your sight. Ever.

7. Be firm.

When a child throws a tantrum or won't do as he's told, you may fear you can't handle it. You can. You're bigger and wiser than he is (even though it may not feel that way!). Be fair, kind, calm, and patient. But be firm. What you say goes.

8. Get in the spirit.

Really play with the kids. Make them laugh. Make yourself laugh, too! The kids will fuss less, and you'll all have a lot more fun.

Boys

My best friend means so-o-o much to me! But now that we're getting older, she is getting into boys. It seems like they are more important than I am!

Erika

When a good friend goes boy crazy, it can feel like a true betrayal. But the real danger to your friendship isn't that boys will become more important to this girl than you are. (After all, she'll still want girlfriends—to giggle with at sleepovers, to confide in, and more!) The real danger is that the two of you are beginning to have different interests. Your friend may find she has more fun with girls who are "into boys," like she is. *You* may find you have more fun with girls who aren't.

For now, do everything you've always done with your friend. But be sure to keep friendships alive with other girls, too. That way, if you two do grow apart, you'll have somewhere else to turn.

Dear *Help!*,

I told a friend
about a boy I like. I thought I could
trust her, but the next day everyone
in class knew about it.

betrayed

Your friend shouldn't have done this. But
the truth is, secrets about boys are the
kind almost nobody keeps. They're too
much fun to tell. From now on, whenever
you open your mouth to tell a friend about
a boy you like, picture your secret on the
chalkboard. If that doesn't bother you,
go ahead and tell. If it does, keep the
news to yourself.

Dear *Help!*,

There's this boy at school that I like.
He's cute, funny, and nice. But I'm
not sure how to tell him that
I like him. How can I tell him?

Puzzled

Easy! You don't need to. If there's a girl
you really like, do you make a big deal
of saying "I like you" to her? Probably
not. You talk to her. You sit next to her
at lunch. You ask her to do things. That's
how one person shows she likes another.
Do the same things with this boy. He'll
get the message. You'll gain a friend, too.

5

Brothers & Sisters

Dear *Help!*,

My sister drives me nuts! I need some plan to get back at her. Here are the things she does to me:

1. She puts mayflies in my bed.
2. She puts fake bugs in my slippers.
3. She comes into my room when I tell her not to, and then when I ask her to go away she says, "It's a free country."

I can't talk to her because she'll destroy me before I say a word. Believe me, I've tried!

Caroline

Bad news, Caroline: "Getting back" at someone just about never works. If you do something nasty to your sister, next time you'll find *real* bugs in your slippers instead of fake ones.

Try this instead: do something *so* nice for your sister that she won't be able to believe it. She'll go crazy wondering what you're really up to. In the meantime the fighting might die down enough that you two could actually imagine being friends.

Dear *Help!*,

My brother is my best friend, but when he has friends over he acts like I'm not there. Sometimes I go in my room and cry.

Very Hurt!

It sounds as if your brother wants some privacy with his friends. Let him have it, and try to find something fun to do on your own. This can be hard, but not as hard as living with a brother who thinks you're a pest. Guaranteed: he'll be happier to see you at dinner if you haven't followed him around all afternoon.

Brothers & Sisters

Dear *Help!*,

My mom and dad never hear my side of the story when I get into fights with my sisters. Right away it is my fault. Take my word, it is not easy being the oldest.

FED UP

True. It isn't easy. Adults sometimes expect an older kid to be more patient than they are themselves. But the fact is that fighting is a bad way to solve a disagreement. Your parents don't *care* what caused the fight. They're unhappy there was a fight to begin with.

Try this: wait till everyone has cooled down—including you. Then talk to your parents privately. Don't say, "It was all Jenny's fault because she tore my notebook!" In fact, don't say the word "fault" at all. Instead, try to solve the problem. Say, "Jenny comes into my room, even though I tell her not to. Can you help me?"

Then do what they suggest. Your parents will see that you're really *trying* to get along with your sisters. The next time there's trouble, they'll be less quick to come down on *you*.

Dear *Help!*,

My sister pretends she's a cat. She'll answer the phone and say, "Meow?" She's been doing this since February, and I think I'm going to go mad!

Mary

Well, you can't hide her under a bucket, and you can't turn her into somebody else. So look at it this way: no sister is *purr*-fect. At least yours seems friendly, and she's not going to keep this up forever. Every girl wants to be able to express herself— even little sisters. Her family should be the last to tell her she can't.

9

Bullies

Dear *Help!*,

The boy next door always kicks me and pulls my hair. I'm afraid if I fight back, he might hurt me even more. If I tell his parents, he'll get punished, but he'll still beat me up. What should I do?

Scared

Tell. Talk to your own parents first. They can talk to this boy's parents or come with you when you do. This boy is never going to be the ideal neighbor. But if he knows you won't cover up for him, he'll think twice before he hurts you again.

Dear *Help!*,

There are two girls who use me, and it hurts. They ask me for money or something, and say, "Do it or I won't be your friend." I've refused them a few times, and it turned into a war. Usually I give them what they want. I don't know what to do!

Used

What awful girls! There is absolutely no reason you should put up with this. Next time they come around, tell them no. You don't need to be afraid of them. They can call you names. They can yell. They can stomp their feet. But take away their friendship? Hardly! Their friendship is something they've never given you— and judging from their actions, it isn't worth much.

Cartwheels

Dear *Help!*,

Whatever I do I cannot turn a cartwheel. I've been trying to learn for about a year. I'm nine, and all my friends can turn one. Even my six-year-old brother can turn one better than I can.

Trying to turn

Get your body ready.
You'll need strong arms and good flexibility. Ask a Phys. Ed. teacher to recommend exercises that will help you stretch and build strength.

READY?

Then brush up on your handstands. Practice leaning forward like this, keeping one leg straight.

Then kick your legs up into a handstand and hold it, leaning against the wall. Have a parent stand by to help.

Now try a cartwheel. **It's really the same old handstand, only sideways.**

Count 1. **Reach down. Place your hand down sideways instead of straight ahead.**

Count 2. **Kick your feet up over your head, keeping your back straight. Your arms and legs are like the spokes of a big wheel.**

Count 3. **Your first foot touches.**

Count 4. **Your second foot touches. Ta-da! You're done!**

Caught Between Friends

Dear *Help!*,

I have two best friends, but they absolutely hate each other! I invited both to my birthday party, and they told each other off. I feel like I'm in a tug-of-war.

Stretched between 2 friends!!

Are these two fighting over you? If so, try to calm their jealousy by telling each one how much you care about her. At the same time, make a few things clear:

(a) You aren't going to drop either friend just because they can't get along.

(b) You'll respect these girls' feelings by spending time with them separately and not playing favorites.

(c) They should respect *your* feelings by not fighting when you're around.

Dear *Help!*,

I have two friends, Sarah and Elizabeth. I like both of them a lot, but Sarah is always saying mean things about Elizabeth. If I say I don't agree, Sarah might not like me anymore. So usually I say, "I know what you mean."

Perplexed

The next time Sarah makes a mean remark about Elizabeth, tell her flat out you disagree. If she gets mad, say you don't think a girl should say bad things about a friend behind her back. You wouldn't speak badly of Sarah. And you're not about to speak badly of Elizabeth, either.

Chatterbox

Dear *Help!*,

My best friend and I sit right next to each other, but she talks too much during class. Then we get in trouble. I tell her not to talk to me when we're working, or when the teacher's talking, but she seems to forget.

Worried

Tell your friend you're really worried about this. Let her know that you're absolutely, positively going to stop talking—even if she doesn't. The next time she talks to you in class, don't answer. She can't have a conversation by herself.

If this doesn't work, there's still one thing that will: Speak to your teacher privately and ask him to move you to another seat.

Cheating

Dear *Help!*,

My friend gets good grades. The problem is that to get those good grades, she cheats. I've seen her. I'm afraid to tell the teacher because my friend might dump me, and nobody else will want to be my friend because I'm a tattletale.

Miffed

Make up your mind to talk to her. Tell this girl straight out that you know what she's doing and it's wrong. Be prepared: she'll probably be mad. Cheaters tell themselves all kinds of lies about why their dishonesty "isn't so bad." But she may also feel ashamed and scared enough to stop—and you won't have had to tell on her to get her to do it.

17

Daredevils

Dear *Help!,*

Some of my friends are really daring. They ask me to do things that might get me in trouble. I don't want to do them, but I have to, or my friends will call me a chicken.

Cheryl

If you don't want to do something, don't do it. *You're* the best judge of what's right for you. If your friends call you a chicken, ignore them. They're turkeys to bully you.

Divorce

Dear *Help!*,

My parents are getting a divorce.
They say everything will stay the
same. I know things will change!
I like it when they're together. I'm
really mad at them. They didn't
even think of me!

mad

Things *will* change. You're right. You may
not like all the changes, either, and it's
natural to be angry about that. But don't
think your parents didn't give you a
thought. Most parents worry about their
kids a lot before divorcing, and do what
they do because they truly believe it's for
the best. That *doesn't* mean you have to
agree with them. And you can tell them
honestly just how mad you feel. Just
don't retreat into your anger and close
the door. Don't lock up your love for
them—or lock out their love for you.

Divorce

Dear *Help!*,

My parents just split up. It's hard
to tell my friends why my dad's not
here. I'm afraid I'll start to cry.

American girl age 10

There's a storm of grief and fear and
anger in your chest. You may feel
ashamed and embarrassed, too. Talking
with a friend can let all these feelings
out. Pick a quiet time and place to tell
the news to a girl you really care about.
And don't be ashamed to cry! You've got
a lot to cry about. Afterward, you'll feel
less alone, and that will help.

Dear *Help!*,

My parents are divorced. My dad's
always saying mean things about my
mom and trying to be the best.

Confused

Your dad is wrong to do this. Don't get
into an argument about whether what
he's saying about your mom is true.
Instead, the next time he says something mean about her, tell him his words
are hurting you. Tell him you love him,
but let him know that if he loves you,
he should be more considerate of how
you feel.

Dear *Help!*,

My parents are divorced and my dad got transferred to Indiana. Now twice a month I have to go to my dad's. I love my dad, but three hours in a car every other weekend is enough! It's been two years since he moved, and I'm tired of it. I don't want my dad to be sad, but I can't help it. I just don't like that drive.

Torn in Two

Traveling back and forth can be hard—*very*. Next time you visit your dad, talk to him about the problem. Could you go less often but stay a little longer sometimes? Could your dad spend the weekend in your town now and then? Or is there something that would make the car trips more fun—like taking a friend along for the weekend? Think hard, and ask your dad to think with you. See how many ideas you come up with, and then pick one or two to try.

Divorce

Dear *Help!*,

My best friend's parents are separated and will probably get a divorce. She never talks about it at school, but she says she cries herself to sleep every night. What can I do to comfort her?

Omaha Girl

Include your friend in all the fun you can. Right now, her house is clearly a sad place to be. She may be less interested in talking about her troubles than she is in getting away from them.

Of course, if this girl *does* want to talk about her family, you should be ready to listen. Reassure her that it's O.K. to cry. Don't say anything bad about either of her parents. And never, ever repeat anything she says. Do this, and you're a true friend.

If It Happens in Your House:

Over half the marriages in the United States end in divorce. That doesn't mean you have to like it. But it does mean lots of other girls have gone through the same thing. Remember this on days you're dying of sadness. If other girls can survive divorce, you can, too.

Dopey Presents

Dear *Help!*,

Sometimes my parents and grand-parents give me clothing that I really think is dopey and ugly. I don't want to hurt their feelings, so I say I like it. This happens a lot. What should I do?

Rebecca

When you get a gift you don't like, thank the person as warmly as if you did. Later on, gently tell your mom or dad you'd prefer something else and ask if you can exchange it. Most adults don't want to spend money on things a kid really won't use. So be honest, but be polite.

Fat

Dear *Help!*,

I'm always getting teased about my weight. My brother calls me things like Porker and Big Bacon. The worst part is, I can't seem to lose the weight. When kids tease me, I not only feel fat, I feel stupid, because they think I don't know the weight is there. Do you know any ways to lose weight besides dieting?

Too Heavy

Bodies come in all sizes and shapes. Some girls are naturally heavier than others, and are healthy and attractive that way. You need to know what weight is right *for you.* So ask your mom to go with you to a doctor. The three of you can discuss just what to do. Will you need to "go on a diet"? Not exactly. Eating cottage cheese for two weeks isn't going to do you a bit of good. But eating healthy foods all year? And getting some exercise? Now *that* could make all the difference in the world.

Dear *Help!*,

I have a friend, Debbie, who is always saying that she's ugly and fat when she's really not. She's very, very pretty and is very, very slender. I try to tell her but she won't believe me.

Anne in Virginia

Your friend may be putting you on, just pretending to be modest to encourage compliments. Or she may truly lack confidence. But she may also be in the early stages of an eating disorder. This is an illness in which a girl believes she's too heavy and starves herself to the point that it can threaten her life. Think: Does your friend go on extreme diets? Is she moody? Secretive? Does she go overboard on exercise? Have you ever seen her throw up on purpose? Does she spend a lot of time in the bathroom after a meal? If the answer to several of these questions is yes, you or one of your parents should talk to the school nurse. Your friend may need professional help.

Fickle Friends

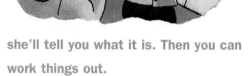

Dear *Help!*,

I have a good friend in my class—
sometimes! One day we're best
buddies, but then she doesn't like
me anymore. It's like a light switch,
on and off, on and off. My other
friends say she's using me. What
should I do?

Mixed Up

Ask her about it nicely. Say, "Why didn't
you talk to me during lunch? Did I
do something that made you mad?" If
she's really your friend, she must have
a reason for "turning off" to you, and
she'll tell you what it is. Then you can
work things out.

And if she *can't* tell you why she
ignores you, or denies that she does?
Then the sign reads: **B-E-W-A-R-E.** She's
treating you badly, and she's not being
honest. The last thing you want is a
friend who hurts your feelings again
and again.

Fights & Friends

My friends and I always get into fights. It happens so suddenly. One person starts ignoring another person, and before we know it we're all in the fight. I hate it. Help!

Kate in Missouri

You can't control all these different friends, but you *can* control yourself. Don't take sides just because sides are forming. Don't fuel the fight by carrying gossip between groups. Be friendly to everybody, and let the storm blow on through.

Forgiving

Dear *Help!,*

My friend's mom was driving in her car with my friend and hit my dog and killed him. I don't want to have to forgive them, and I don't know if I can.

Hurt

When something terrible happens, a person often needs somebody to be mad at. The sadness is so hard to bear! But anger can weigh you down like a two-ton rock. You *need* to forgive your friend and her mom, as much for your sake as for theirs.

Tell your friend you need time to get over your dog's death. If you can't tell her to her face, write a note. You *know* it was an accident. While you grieve for your dog in the days ahead, remind yourself of accidents you yourself have caused and how horrible you felt about them. As you accept your loss, your anger will cool, and with luck forgiveness will follow.

Foster Kid

Dear *Help!*,

I'm a foster child, and I just moved into a new neighborhood. All the kids make fun of me because of my position in life. When I go outside to play they never come over, and they avoid me like I have a disease. How can I show them I'm just like they are?

Disease Girl

No way do you have a disease! It's the other kids who are showing unhealthy signs—of ignorance.

Talk to your foster parents. They know the block better than you do, and may have all sorts of ideas that could help. For starters, perhaps they know which of these kids would respond well to an invitation to do something special with you. If you can make a friend of one girl, she can tell the others that you don't come from another planet.

Grandparents

Dear *Help!*,

My grandmother died a few weeks ago. Sometimes I see my mom crying. I loved my grandmother with all my heart. Sometimes I cry too. What can I do to stop thinking about my grandmother?

A sad girl

Do everything you usually do: go to school, participate in activities, see friends. These things will keep you from dwelling too much on your grandmother's death. But at other, quieter times you *will* think of her, and it's right that you do. Your sadness is like a door you have to pass through for your life to return to normal. When it does, the memories that made you cry will bring you happiness instead, and your grandmother will live again, in your heart.

Dear *Help!*,

My grandpa has been sick for two months, and my grandma is staying with us. We love each other, but we just don't get along.

At the End of My Rope

P.S. I tried talking with her. She began to cry and said maybe she should go home.

Ask your mom to be the peacemaker. Make a list of things that cause trouble between you and your grandmother— things like "She says mean things about my clothes" or "She says I'm rude." Then go through them with your mom one by one. Listen to your mom's ideas about what you can do to make things better. Ask if she'll talk to your grandmother as well. Then work at getting along one day at a time. Walls between people build up little by little—brick by brick. They can come down the same way.

Hair

Dear *Help!*,

My mom is always nagging at me to do something nicer with my hair. I don't know how to do much with my hair. What should I do?

M. Z.

2. Fancy up your ponytail. Gather the top layer of hair into a small ponytail.

1. If you have long hair, move your ponytail to a new spot on your head. Or try more than one ponytail.

Then gather the next layer of hair and add that to the first. Then gather the rest.

3. Make one long ponytail. Braid it. Twist it into a bun, tuck in the end, and pin it.

5. Make two small braids. Pin them on top of your head with hairpins, tucking in the ends.

4. Or make two ponytails, braid, and do the same thing.

6. Make one small braid by your ear. Wear it straight or pull it over your head like a headband and pin it.

Hair

7. If you have short hair, pull your hair back on one side of your face. Twist it. Then fasten it with a barrette. Wear it that way or do the same thing on the other side, too.

8. Make your own fancy barrettes. Get a variety of ribbons from a fabric store: polka-dot, striped, plaid, plain. Tie the ribbons onto plain metal barrettes.

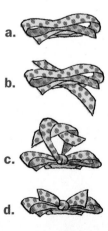

a.

b.

c.

d.

Hogged by a Friend

Dear *Help!*,

I have this friend and she is hogging me. I can't do anything with my other friends unless she's with me.

Hogged

Tell this girl you feel hogged and don't like it. Be kind. Tell her that her friendship is important to you. Tell her that your caring about other girls doesn't mean you care less about her. But let her know you like having lots of friends. If she continues to try to keep you all to herself, she's only going to lose you for good.

Home Alone

Dear *Help!,*

I'm afraid to stay home alone. I'm always thinking a burglar or a murderer will come to my house. When the doorbell rings I'm afraid to open the door. How can I stop being afraid?

Old but Scared

You have a lot of control over how safe you are. The trick is making yourself believe it! There are a number of simple rules that you should follow when you're home alone. A few are listed on the next page. Talk with your parents about others. Type them into a list that you keep near the phone. A stranger at the door or on the phone should be a lot less scary if you know for sure what to do.

Of course it may also be that you're just not ready to stay home alone yet. That's perfectly O.K. Tell your parents how you feel. Together you may be able to figure out another choice.

When you're home alone:

1. Don't answer the door unless you've looked through a peephole or out a window and recognize the person. If it's a stranger, don't open the door. Ever. If there's no way to see who's at the door, keep it shut and call, "Who is it?"

2. Meter readers, repairmen, delivery people—if your parents didn't tell you to expect them, keep the door shut. They can always come back another time.

3. If someone calls and asks for your dad or mom, say that he or she can't come to the phone right now and offer to take a message. Don't say you're alone. If the caller seems too nosy, hang up. Then phone one of your parents and describe the call.

4. Know your neighbors. Keep their numbers next to the phone, along with your parents' work numbers and other emergency numbers. As long as you've got these, you're not totally alone.

Homesick

Dear *Help!*,

I don't like spending the night at friends' houses. I get a funny feeling in my stomach. I can only think about my family and house. Sometimes I go into the bathroom and cry. I end up coming home and feeling confused and humiliated.

Homesick

Don't be ashamed! This is a problem lots of girls have.

If a friend invites you to sleep over, tell her the truth. Explain what it's like for you when you don't sleep at home.

If she's not having a party, maybe you can have her sleep at your house instead. If she is, ask if you can go to the first half of the party and have your parents pick you up before bedtime. You'll still get to share in most of the fun.

"I'm SO Embarrassed!"

Dear *Help!*,

At recess I was doing gymnastics near some boys. While I was landing a handspring, my shirt flew up! The boys began to laugh because I didn't have anything on underneath. Now they won't let me forget it.

Miserable in Virginia

They'll forget it themselves eventually. The joke will get old. They'll tease you less often. They'll discover a new way to get a laugh, and get all caught up in something else. In the meantime, be patient, ignore them, and tuck in your shirt.

39

Invitations

Dear *Help!*,

My birthday is coming up, and I want to have a sleepover. The only problem is, I can only invite five girls. I know who I want to invite, but I don't want to hurt my other friends' feelings. I can only have one party.

Not wanting to hurt

Mail the invitations. Giving them out at school is sure to make the uninvited girls feel worse. You should also be careful not to talk about the party in front of girls who aren't included—and to do what you can to encourage your guests not to talk about it, either. If a girl finds out about the party anyway—as often happens— talk to her. Tell her about the limit your parents set, and ask if she will do something fun with you another time. She'll still feel bad, but she'll also know you're still her friend.

Dear *Help!*,

Every so often a problem comes up. One of my friends calls to see if I can play. Then later a different friend calls to see if I can play. How do I pick who to play with if I know I'll have more fun with the friend who called last?

Mixed Up

If you told the first friend you would go with her, you should do it. Be true to your word.

Jealousy

Dear *Help!*,

My best friend is good at *everything!* She's so smart. I'm really jealous. She always gets A+'s and special awards, which makes me feel dumb. Whenever I find something I'm good at, she does it five billion times better.

Jealous in Connecticut

The writer William Shakespeare called jealousy the green-eyed monster, and he had it right. It can really mess up your life if you let it. Already jealousy has made you feel bad about yourself and resent your best friend. And it's done

nothing to help you get an A+, either. Drive a stake through its heart! The truth is, everyone has special talents. Don't overlook your own in a desire to have your friend's. If you enjoy something—math, painting, you name it—throw yourself into it with all your heart. You'll discover what fun it is being yourself—and no award can top that.

Jitters

Dear *Help!*,

At school, every year we have tryouts for a play. You have to sing in front of people and dance. I really want to try out, but I'm afraid.

Scared

Practice. Practice alone. Practice in front of a mirror. Practice in front of the dog. Practice in front of your family and your friends. Nothing builds confidence like knowing what you're going to do.

And if you still feel nervous at try-outs? No problem. Nervousness is your body's way of getting you ready for a special event. Nervous energy can turn into creative energy and actually help you do better. When tryouts come, breathe deeply and do your best. If you get a part: great! If you don't, start planning for the next tryout. Sooner or later, you'll land the role you want.

Left Out

Dear *Help!*,

I have two friends. When I'm with one of them everything is O.K. But if the other friend comes over, they always leave me out or gang up on me.

K.D.

You've heard it before and it's true: three is often a bad number. Invite your friends over one at a time. Or if the three of you are going somewhere together, bring along a fourth girl or even a fifth. In a bigger group, your two friends will be less likely to pair off. And if they do, you'll still have someone else to be with.

Looking Dumb

I'm afraid to answer questions in class. Some kids are really smart and always get the right answers. Sometimes I think the teacher will embarrass me if I say the wrong thing. One time I raised my hand and said the wrong answer, and the boy in front of me snickered.

Embarrassed

There may be *some* kids who always get the right answers, but there must be more who don't. It's not a big deal when somebody else makes a mistake, is it?

There's no reason to be harder on yourself than you are on the girl at the next desk. So don't crawl into a hole! Raise your hand. If you're wrong—so what? Making mistakes is part of learning. It's laughing at another kid's mistakes that's dumb.

Losing a Friend

Dear *Help!*,

I have a best friend who now sits with the popular girls. I try my hardest to have her notice me, but she ignores me. I have been best friends with her for a long time. What should I do?

Happy before, not anymore

When a girl ignores you again and again, she's telling you she doesn't want to be friends anymore. It can break your heart, but there isn't much you can do about it except find some new friends. Don't say anything angry to this girl. Be as polite to her as you would be to anyone else.

But quit waiting for her to notice you. Sit with some girls you'd like to know better. Make some fun plans with them. Every day, you'll hurt a little less. In the end, another girl will mean as much to you as the first one did. Maybe more.

Making a Friend

Dear *Help!*,

There's this girl in some of my sixth-grade classes, and she never talks to anyone. She looks very nice, and I would like to make friends with her. My only problem is, how do I introduce myself and not feel like a nerd? And how can I get her to like me?

Jennifer

Relax! There's nothing nerdy about being friendly. Work up your courage and say, "Hi! I'm Jennifer." Ask some friendly questions. This girl sounds shy and you do, too. The two of you may feel awkward at first, trying to find things to say. *That's really O.K.* The important thing is that you were friendly to begin with. Just don't make the mistake of trying to impress her by talking big. Be yourself, and she'll like you fine.

Mean Friends

Dear *Help!*,

I have a friend who is not nice to me at all. She always gets mad if I don't do what she wants. And she talks about me. She will say bad things, then say, "Just kidding!" I get so mad at her!

Katie

You're right to be mad! Don't be a doormat for a friend who treats you poorly. Tell this girl how you feel. If she wants your friendship, she's got to treat you with respect. Tell her you'll walk away the next time she acts badly—and then do it, even if it's very hard. She'll learn you mean what you say.

Messy

Dear *Help!*,

I just can't keep my room clean. I try and try. Every time I clean it, it gets even messier. I do not like to live in a room where there isn't enough room to walk.

The Messiest Person in Seattle

Less stuff means less mess. Get some grocery bags. Mark them "Give Away," "Garbage," "Basement," "Garage Sale," and so on. Now march over to that closet. Pull things out one by one. Be honest with yourself. If you don't wear it, put it in a bag. If you don't play with it, put it in a bag. If it could be stored in another room—*boom.* Into a bag. Put on some music and sing out loud while you work. Sort the things in the rest of your room, too. The more stuff you put into the bags and get out of there, the better.

HELP!

Then...

Messy

Use boxes, baskets, jars, crates, and cans to contain and organize the rest.

Collections go on a shelf, not on the dresser.

Hang your beads on the bulletin board.

WC MQ

Cereal boxes, cut diagonally and decorated, hold magazines and papers.

Use bookends.

GIVE AWAY

TRASH

TRASH

Little boxes and coffee cans organize drawer

hair scrunchie

Middle School

Dear *Help!*,

This year I'll be going to middle school. I don't know what to think. I'm always looking forward to new adventures, but I'm scared at the same time. I mean, what about the older kids and showers and locker combinations. I don't know...

Lindsay

You're not alone. Chances are, every kid in your class feels a lot like you. Do this: Talk to some girls who started middle school last year. What was fun about it? What was hard? What would have made the hard things easier? Ask every question you have. You should also be sure to attend any orientation events the school offers. And make a point of walking around the building with your mom or dad. You'll be surprised how much better you'll feel just knowing where the lunchroom is!

Money

Whenever I get money, I spend it on things I don't really want or need—even though I meant to save for something I really did want. Please help me think of a way to save money.

Wanting to Save

1. Get two cans. Mark them "Save" and "Spend." When you get your allowance or are paid for a job you've done, divide the money equally between the cans. You can take money out of the "Save" can just four times a year. No cheating!

2. Don't take money with you to the mall. If you don't have it with you, you can't spend it.

3. When you spend money on candy and little stuff, save the wrappers. Collect them in a clear jar. It will remind you of just where all that money has gone—and how little you got for it.

Money

Dear *Help!*,

My mother started a business, and now we never have any extra money. She says it takes a while for a business to start, but she's been saying that for the last year! All my friends have money for roller-skating and stuff on weekends. I feel left out.

Nicole

Well, you can't wish away your mom's business. Instead, try thinking up fun things to do with your friends that don't cost money. You can also earn the money you want by starting a business of your own. Many girls babysit, of course. But you could sell things or run errands—there are lots of possibilities. You'll find it feels good to have money you earned yourself—which is probably why your mom started that business in the first place!

Things you can sell—Start with necklaces you've beaded yourself. ✦ Or buy a variety of ribbons at a fabric store, cut them into lengths, put several colors together in a packet, and sell them to girls to wear in their hair. ✦ Have a one-girl garage sale and sell old toys. ✦ Sell popcorn at soccer games, apples at football games, homemade lemonade at swim meets. ✦ String cranberries and popcorn, and sell the strands as decorations at Christmas. ✦ Always charge more than your materials cost you, but not a lot more. ✦

Services you can offer to friends and neighbors—Mow lawns, weed gardens, rake leaves, shovel snow. ✦ Walk dogs. Wash dogs. ✦ Wash cars and windows. ✦ Help with recycling. ✦ Do dusting. ✦ Take in mail, water plants, and care for animals while people are on vacation. ✦ Run errands on your bike. ✦ Tutor. ✦ Start a playgroup with a friend where parents can leave toddlers for a few hours each week. ✦ Make treasure hunts for kids' parties. ✦ Make a haunted house and charge admission. ✦ Wrap your head in a towel and tell funny fortunes. ✦

Moving

Dear *Help!*,

My parents want to move and I truly don't. I don't want to leave my friends or my school. I am scared to death about it.

Against the moving trucks

Saying good-bye is a lot easier if you've arranged a time to say hello again. If you aren't moving far, plan a return visit. If you are, promise your friends that you'll write and call—and then do it.

You might also spend some time before you leave thinking about your life in your new home: How are you going to decorate your new room? What clubs are you going to join at school? What places do you want to visit after you move? Make all the plans you can. You'll dread the move less if you have things to look forward to. And with projects to do and places to go, you'll feel more at home when you get to the new house.

Nail-biting

Dear *Help!,*

I have a bad habit. I bite my nails. I've tried to stop but nothing helps. Everybody else has pretty nails, but mine are little tiny things.

Mad at myself

1. Most drugstores sell a product for girls like you. It's like nail polish, only the taste is horrible. Use it daily. And *keep* using it as your nails begin to grow.

2. Wear gloves while you're watching TV, reading, or hanging out at home. It may look goofy, but it will help.

3. Ask your mom or dad if they'll treat you to a manicure at a hair salon if you don't bite your nails for a week. You'll enjoy working toward a reward, and once your nails are pretty you'll want to keep them that way.

4. Remember, a habit like this is hard to break, so don't let setbacks stop you. If you bite new nails, start over. Your determination will make you succeed.

New Baby

Dear *Help!*,
Ever since my mom had a baby, my parents have ignored me. They only notice me when they tell me to do something. I'm always helping out with the baby and around the house.

Invisible child

What you need are "chore chats." If you're folding laundry with your dad, fill him in on your friends while you do it. If you're drying dishes while mom feeds the baby, tell her about your music class while you work. Your parents love you as much as they always have. They just don't have time to show it. Life will get easier as the baby gets older. But for now you have a better chance of getting their attention if you don't compete with the baby. They'll enjoy your talks and be grateful for your help. Who knows? They may even find a quiet moment to say so.

Not a Baby Anymore

Dear *Help!*,

My mother is turning into my jailer. I don't think she knows she's got to let go of me sometime. I'm just about going insane! For heaven's sake, I'm ten already! She's not letting me grow up!

Mad at Mom

You can't change your mom's opinions about what's safe or what's appropriate for girls your age. (And the fights will only get bigger if you try.) What you *can* do is show your mom you're mature and responsible—about chores, about homework, even about these disagreements themselves. Remember, nothing makes you *look* more like a baby than stomping and yelling. So when your mom says no, stay calm and listen. You'll be a lot more successful in explaining why you think as you do. Chances are, she won't change her mind, but she'll be impressed by your behavior—and eventually that will help.

Pets

Dear *Help!*,

I really want another pet, other than what I have now—a rabbit. What I really want is a dog, but I'd be happy with even a little goldfish. Anything but a rabbit that doesn't do anything but just sit there and sniff at you. My parents don't think I'm responsible. I'm plenty responsible!

Doggone!

Hmm. It's clear you've got to prove yourself to your parents. Try this: Spend at least two months taking very good care of that rabbit. Feed it, give it fresh water, keep the cage clean. Do all this (a) without complaining, (b) without being nagged, and (c) without asking for a different pet. These actions will show far better than words just how responsible you are. Then try asking again. You may be happily surprised.

Dear *Help!*,

We got a new puppy about a month ago, and my parents are ready to sell him already! Just because he jumps all over us and digs up the flowers and chases the car up and out of the driveway doesn't mean we should sell him *already.*

Desperate

Your puppy's being a puppy! He can't behave like a full-grown dog any more than your two-year-old sister can behave like a grownup. Here's your best hope: Tell your parents that if they'll give the puppy time to grow up and settle down, you'll give him the other thing he needs: training. Your puppy's vet can offer advice on dog-training. A library will have books on it, too. Work with your puppy every day. He'll soon learn the rules.

Picked Last

Dear *Help!*,

In sports I always get picked last because people think I'm slow and can't do anything. I may not be quick, but I have skills! The others put me in places where I don't get to do anything. *Ashley*

Being picked last can make you feel as if somebody's hung a sign around your neck that says you're no good. But you're right to say speed isn't everything. Skill in sports is a combination of practice, coordination, and attitude. If you practice and play hard, you should do well. Don't worry for now about what position you play. Just play it as well as you can, and eventually kids may notice you're better than they thought.

Picked On

Dear *Help!*,

All the kids pick on me because I'm different. They say I have cooties and call me names. I keep getting the same advice: "Just ignore it." "Laugh and pretend it's funny." Can you give me different advice?

Not Laughing

You can talk to some of these kids individually, and tell them what they know in their hearts—that what they're doing is wrong and cruel. You can also talk to your teacher and your parents. With teasing this mean, an adult should get involved and call a halt. Above all, don't let these kids make you feel bad about yourself. Look them in the eye! A lot of creative, talented people were picked on for being "different" when they were kids. Besides, your differences express who you are. And it's the girls who are true to themselves who will be the happiest in the end.

Popularity

Dear *Help!,*

I don't need to be really popular. Then again, I don't want to be a down-in-the-dirt nobody, either. What do I do?

Heather

Look into your heart. Who are the girls who make you feel happy to be yourself? Who are the girls who treat you with kindness and respect? Who are the girls who don't change friends every minute? Who are the girls you can trust?

Got the answer? *These* are your friends. Be true to them. They may be "popular" or they may be "nobodies." What other kids think of them doesn't matter a smidge. Neither does what other kids think of *you* for being their friend.

Dear *Help!*,

There is an "in crowd" at our school. They think they are better than everyone else and put other people down. My friends and I try to be friends with them, but every time we try, they either tease us or ignore us.

Teased in Tennessee

Why are you trying to be friends with these girls? They don't sound nice, and it's clear they make you feel crummy. Forget them. If they want to amuse themselves by being mean—that's their choice. But don't set yourself up for a snub.

Practicing

Dear *Help!*,

I play the violin. I really like it, but I hate practicing. I don't want to quit. What should I do?

Jessica

Practicing is always easier if you're working toward a goal, like a recital. Try giving a monthly concert for your family. Or find an opportunity to listen to a violinist a level above you and decide you're going to learn to play a certain piece as well as she does. Talk to your teacher, too, about setting other goals, or learning pieces you particularly like.

All these things will help. The truth is, though, that learning *can* be frustrating—and practicing *isn't* always going to be fun. But it is rewarding. VERY. Your instincts are right. Stick with it. You will absolutely, positively be glad you did.

Procrastination

Dear *Help!*,

I have a project I'm supposed to be finishing, but I've hardly started. My mom says my problem is procrastination, or putting things off till later. I've tried writing calendars and schedules, but it doesn't work.

Hopeless

You don't need a calendar. You just need to sit down and start on that project—*now!* And here's an idea that will make you do it: Ask your parents to put your allowance into quarters. For every hour you procrastinate instead of doing your project, they should put a quarter into a jar marked "I'LL DO IT LATER." Once a quarter goes into the jar, you can't have it till your project's done.

Racism

Dear *Help!*,

I'm eleven years old. I am Korean. Boys at school make fun of me because I'm Oriental. Next time they make fun of me, what should I say? If I tell the teacher, they'll make fun of me because I told on them.

Unhappy

It's not easy to stand up to people like this, so it's important that you ask your parents and your teacher for help. Racist teasing is very, very serious. It's serious because it's so hurtful to kids like you. It's serious because it poisons the whole school by allowing kids to imagine racism has a place there. It shouldn't be ignored or tolerated—ever. Therefore:

1. Try to be brave and speak out. When one of the boys makes a nasty comment about your race, say, "That's a racist thing to say." Your friends should speak out, too. This may make him see his "joke" in a very different light. He may feel ashamed and stop.

2. Tell your parents and your teacher what's going on. *This is not a problem that you should have to handle alone.* The adults are in a better position than you are to stop these boys, and it's in the best interest of every child in your school that they do it.

3. Your parents and your teacher will probably talk to the boys and the boys' parents, and that's good. They may also re-examine whether kids at your school are learning enough about the history of racism and cultures different from their own. Remember, this is a complicated problem that people in this country have been fighting throughout our history. Solutions are difficult, and don't happen overnight.

4. A lot of people—children and grown-ups alike—are afraid to talk about race. They keep their thoughts and feelings hidden under a rock of silence. Don't be one of them! Try to be open about what you see and how you feel, even though that can be hard. Your honesty can get others talking. You'll be doing something important in the fight against racism— and that will feel good.

Shopping

Dear *Help!*,

Here's my problem: my mother picks out my clothes when we go shopping, and she and I have totally different taste in clothes.

Soured on Shopping

If your mom picks out an outfit you really hate, explain nicely what you don't like about it. Then listen to her explain what she does. Is there something else on the racks that will satisfy you both? Or would she pick four or five outfits, and then let you choose among them? If you want one thing badly, you can ask to pay for it with your own money. But don't get hung up arguing about an outfit your mom just plain hates. Compromise. If you don't dig in *your* heels, maybe she won't dig in *hers*, and you'll be a lot more likely to leave happy with what's in the bag.

Sore Loser

Dear *Help!*,

I'm a sore loser. I cry when I lose. I try to hold it in, but I can't!

Annie

Nobody likes to lose, but learning to do it gracefully makes things a whole lot easier. Luckily, you know what's right: you *want* to be a good sport. That desire will soon grow into the self-control you need. For now, if you've got to cry, do it as quickly and privately as you can. Just be sure that when the tears stop, you congratulate the winner as nicely as you would want someone to congratulate you.

Speaking Out

Dear *Help!*,

I know a girl who is always teased. I laugh with everybody else, but I feel so bad! This girl has been teased all her life, and she laughs with people too, even though she must feel bad down in her heart. What should I do to help her?

Sorry and Last

You've probably read books where girls do heroic things like saving someone's life. And you may have wondered what it would be like to be brave like that. Well, here's your chance. Don't go along with the crowd. Tell the teasers that what they're doing is cruel. They may fight back by saying mean things to you. But it will be harder for them next time to pretend this is just a game. You'll need courage to speak out. You'll like yourself, though, if you do. And to at least one girl at school, you'll be a hero in real life.

Spiders

Dear *Help!*,

This might sound silly, but I'm scared of spiders. My mom says just kill them. But spiders look scary!

Audry

True. But think: You are 150 times taller than most spiders. You weigh 10,000 times as much. You're also smarter. It's not much of a contest. Keep that in mind the next time you see a spider skitter across a wall. Don't jump up shrieking. Make yourself move slowly. Keep your voice soft. If you *act* calm, it can help you *feel* calm.

Stepfamilies

Dear *Help!*,

My mom got remarried in July. It seems like she cares more for my stepfather and his kids than she does for me and my sisters.

Depressed

Your mom doesn't love them more than she loves you. It just feels that way because you have to share her. Right now, everyone is having to make changes and settle into new relationships. This is all part of what happens when parents remarry and two different families come together. It's natural to feel uncertain and jealous—even angry—at a time like this. The important thing is to talk to your mom about how you feel. That way, she can try to help.

Dear *Help!*,

My dad always brings his new wife to my swim meets even though I tell him that I don't want her there. I don't like her because she was the cause of my parents' divorce. I think she's only pretending to be nice. Should I get revenge or just ignore them?

Mad In Michigan

Neither. By bringing his new wife to your meets, your dad is telling you he's not going to let you ignore her. If you try to "get revenge" by insulting your stepmother or hurting her feelings, you'll damage your relationship with your dad. You'll also damage yourself, by teaching yourself to say and do mean things. You are mistress of your own heart, and nobody can make you like your stepmother, or even forgive her. But don't give hate a permanent home in your heart. If you turn this relationship into a war, the person hurt worst will be you.

Teacher's Pet

Dear *Help!*,

I have always made straight A's.
Everyone calls me a goody-goody or
teacher's pet. I just try to do my best,
but they make it seem like it's bad.

Perfect

Teasing like this often comes from jealousy. Being good in school is something
to be very, very proud of. At the bottom
of their hearts, the kids who pester you
know that. Ask a friend if there's anything
you do that makes the others think you're
a show-off. If there is, change it. But
never, ever play dumb when you're not.

Teacher Trouble

Dear *Help!*,

My teacher is so strict! She never smiles. She reminds me of a rain cloud. She gives out checks if you make one itsy bitsy teeny weeny mistake.

Girl who needs a new teacher

Never smiles? Yikes! Well, study hard, do your homework, and whenever you finish a paper or a test, read it over before you hand it in. This will cut down on little mistakes. You'll also know you've done your best, and that's all any teacher can ask.

At the same time, keep an open mind, if you can. This teacher could surprise you and turn out to be less crabby than she seems right now.

#@!!*&%!!!

Dear Help!,

I have a horrible temper. A day doesn't pass without me yelling at my parents or my little brother. I always wish that I could take back everything I said.

frustrated with myself

If you can't control your emotions, practice controlling your body instead. When you feel yourself beginning to blow, say "I have to be alone" and leave the room. Just start walking and don't stop. March up and down a hallway. Stomp around the basement. Go outside and walk around the house. Talk out loud. Do anything that helps you let off steam. You'll cool down eventually. Then if you want to take back something you said . . . do.

Too Short

Dear *Help!*,

I'm in desperate need of advice. I am eleven years old. So what? I am four feet three inches and wear a size one shoe, that's what! I am being teased every minute of my life. If it's not one person, it's another. I'm starting to get very frustrated.

Small in San Jose

P.S. I tried to talk to my teachers. They said, "You know, you guys have to work that out." Well, no kidding. There isn't a thing in the world wrong with being short. Don't let anyone make you think there is. Here's a ditty that will remind you of that—and put the teasers in their place:

My hands are little,
my skirt petite,
I wear teeny shoes
on tiny feet,
But nothing about me
is quite as small
As a kid who has
no manners at all.

Ugly

Dear *Help!*,

Some days I look really ugly. My friends and I all think so. I know beauty is in the eyes of the beholder, but I still want to be prettier!

Dog face

Prettiness has less to do with a person's features (stuff like the size of your nose and the shape of your eyes) than you might think. What really matters is a healthy look, cleanliness, personal style—and personality. If you really believe in yourself, and beam confidence in your eyes and smile, you're attractive whether you're a beauty or not. So take care of your skin. Wash your hair. But don't, *don't,* DON'T spend time looking in the mirror, searching your face for mistakes. Go do something that makes you happy. Your face will shine with its own light.

Unwanted Friends

Dear *Help!*,

I have a big little problem, and its name is Barbara. She really wants to be my friend. But I don't want to be her friend. No matter where I go she finds me. What should I do?

Frustrated

What you shouldn't do is say: "I don't want to be your friend." After all, there's no reason to be *un*friendly to someone who's friendly to you. You simply don't want Barbara to stick to you like glue. So tell her it seems as if she's following you around. As kindly as you can, say you feel you have no privacy with your other friends. Then be patient. Try to remember that though your situation is tough, Barbara's is worse. She won't keep this up forever. Sooner or later, she'll give up hope and offer her friendship to someone who is glad to have it.

Working Parents

Dear *Help!*,

My mom has been looking for a job, and it seems she may have found one. If she really gets the job, there will be a lot of changes to be made. I'm not sure I'm ready for them!

Unsure

Families grow and change over time, just like the people in them. Right now, you may be worried about what you will do after school or about your new responsibilities around the house. That's natural, and you should talk about these things with your parents, so they can help. Remember, though, your mom's going to work is one more stage in your family's life—like the day you started kindergarten or the day your sister left for college. What seems scary and difficult today will be routine tomorrow.

Dear *Help!*,

My dad works a lot, so my mom and my sister and I hardly ever see him. We all miss spending time together.

Troubled Girl

Say so. Tell your parents you'd like to have an official Family Huddle every week. A Family Huddle is anything that brings all of you together to have fun and talk. One week it could be doing a jigsaw puzzle. The next week it could be taking a walk after dinner. The important thing is that everyone knows when Family Huddle will be and plans for it.

"You Throw Like a Girl"

My teacher is very sexist against girls. Just today, he said to a girl named Catherine after she threw the football, "You throw like a girl." I said, "*What?*" And he said, "Oh, our little women's rights movement person is back there." You know, and so do I, that you can't talk back to teachers, but what do I do?

Elizabeth

Talk to your parents. Ask if they will come with you to talk to the teacher. They can say to him what seems obvious to you: "A bad throw is not the same thing as a girl's throw. It's insulting to girls to say that it is." Your parents may want to talk to the principal, too. In the meantime, don't let this man change how you play sports or think about yourself. Not one teeny tiny bit.

Dear *Help!*,

I'm the only girl on my basketball team. I'm pretty good at it, too. But the boys never pass me the ball.

Amy in Alabama

It's your coach's job to make sure the team plays as a team. Talk to her. If the boys are hogging the ball, she can tell them they're not allowed to take a shot until they've passed at least once to you. She can also put you into some special plays. Either way, you'll be able to show what you can do. If the boys want to win, they'll learn to let go of the ball.

ZZZZZzzzz (bored!)

Dear *Help!*,

I stay home alone during summer weekdays. I've done everything to keep myself occupied, but it's no use. I'm so-o-o bored. Y'all got any advice?

An extremely bored Texan

1. Don't assume you're stuck in the house because your parents can't drive you places. See what activities your friends and neighbors are signing up for. Maybe you can sign up, too, and hitch a ride. 2. Think: What else interests you? Gymnastics? Science? Earning money? Set yourself a goal and work at home to

achieve it. Don't forget about volunteering, either. Look around: whom can you help? 3. There's nothing worse than eating breakfast with an empty day staring you in the face. Plan ahead. Call friends in advance. 4. Don't wait for something interesting to happen to you. MAKE it happen. You've got a brain that can think up new twists on old games. You've got a fun spirit waiting to throw off the gloom. Put them to work! The truth is, life is full of problems—boredom's just one of them. Learn to find happiness in little things. It's like spinning straw into gold.

Spinning straw into gold—**Paint a friend's toenails at the same time she paints yours.** ✶ Pretend you moved to Mars. Draw a picture of what your bedroom looks like. ✶ **Do the limbo with a friend under the stream of water from a garden hose.** ✶ **Read every book your favorite author ever wrote.** ✶ **Throw a birthday party for a pet.** ✶ **Do a jigsaw puzzle on the porch.** ✶ **Do a favor for a friend.** ✶ Make a frappé. Put in a blender: 1 cup of fresh or frozen strawberries, 2 tablespoons sugar, 1 cup crushed ice, and 1 cup milk. Mix it up. Mmm! ✶

Draw a picture of your brother with your feet. ★ Cook dinner. Play mood music. Be a waiter: take orders. Accept tips. ★ Shoot Ping-Pong balls off soda bottles with a squirt gun. ★ Wake up at dawn, make cinnamon toast, and watch the sun rise. ★ Be fruity. Mold banana beads out of Sculpey clay. Make a banana bracelet. ★ Use gel to give your friend a hairdo from outer space. Have her give you one, too. Run through the sprinkler till it's all washed out. ★ Be a soccer star next fall: work on your skills by kicking a soccer ball in and out of a line of tin cans. ★

Sneak a candy into a friend's pocket. Let her wonder where it came from. ★ Dress up. Pretend you're giving a concert while you practice your instrument. Get up now and then to take a bow. ★ Start a journal. ★ Have a tournament: invite the neighbors to play badminton, croquet, jacks, jump-rope, or charades. ★ Write a letter to your grandparents. Put on lipstick and seal it with a kiss. ★ Lie down on the driveway. Have someone trace around you with chalk. Draw yourself some clothes and a new hairdo. ★ Take the dog for the best walk it's ever had.

Wear sunglasses. Act famous. ☆ Put a picnic cloth on the floor of your room and invite a friend for lunch on a rainy day. ☆ Teach your little brother to dance. ☆ Shoot baskets. ☆ Identify all the trees on your block. ☆ Rearrange the furniture in your room. ☆ Make the world's longest clover chain. Have your mom wear it at dinner. ☆ Get together with your friends for Hawaii Day at the local pool. Hula off the diving board. Wear leis. Drink pineapple juice. ☆ Go for a walk in the rain. ☆ Make a timeline of your life. Put a big fat star on today. ☆

More Help!

You don't have to face your troubles alone. If you need more advice than we've offered here, look around you. Help is there: at home, at school, in the library, at your church or synagogue, in the community.

Talk to your parents. Talk to a teacher. Talk to a counselor at school. Talk to another adult who is close to your family. These people can't solve the problem *for* you, but they can be a big help. If your problem is really serious, an adult can even bring in a professional whose job consists of helping people like you.

Keep in mind that a big problem can't be solved overnight. It's going to take time. If one thing doesn't work, try another. And if *that* doesn't work, try something else. Never, ever give up.

You don't have to face your problems alone!